Memoirs To God

(from An Achilles Heart)

by

Nina L. Toth

Wordclay
1663 Liberty Drive, Suite 200
Bloomington, IN 47403
www.wordclay.com

First published by Wordclay on 4/16/2008

ISBN: 978-0-615-20474-1 (sc)

Printed in the United States of America
Bloomington, Indiana

This book is printed on acid-free paper.

Dedication

This book is dedicated to the Lord, Jesus Christ. To Pastor Bruce Schafer, a good Shepherd who brought true illumination to God's Word. To my children Lauren and Sarah, who brought Love to my existence, and to everyone who believes his life has no purpose.

Contents

Introduction

In writing this book, I am attempting to travel a path of life where the end of the road leads to healing and freedom. I am delving into the recesses of my mind to unearth and slay a dragon—a dragon that has loomed over my life and has taken on many forms. When I refer to this dragon, I am speaking of the enemy of my peace: a destroyer of my dreams and visions. The very one who first planted the idea in my mind that I am inferior and deserve less in life.

In order to carry out a plan for total liberation, I must first recognize the dragon that has tried all my life to depress, oppress, and possess me with its presence. This nemesis, I have discovered, is responsible for the gradual decline to settling for mediocrity in my existence.

In order to dig a well, one must first prime it. Before the well becomes a clean, useful source of water, we must pump all the dirt, debris, and impurities out of the system, and then it will become functional. In a sense, this book is helping me to achieve that very task.

This life can be a constant source of pain and hurt. In this book, I focus on the recipients of that pain, not the contributors, for they are also living a hellish existence. Since all are given a free choice by our heavenly Father, they must also face their own dragons and start to live in truth again.

Writing this book serves as a bridge for me; the other side leads to peace and freedom from the bonds of rejection, hurt, and unforgiveness. As you read this book, should you find yourself on common ground, may you feel the love and compassion of our Lord around and within you. Always know you are not alone. He holds you in His mighty hand.

> Surely He has borne our griefs (sicknesses, weaknesses, and distresses) and carried our sorrows and pains [of punishment], yet we [ignorantly] considered Him stricken, smitten, and afflicted by God [as if with leprosy]. But He was wounded for our transgressions, He was bruised for our guilt and iniquities; the chastisement [needful to obtain] peace and well-being for us was upon Him, and with the stripes [that wounded] Him we are healed and made whole. (Isa. 53:4–5 AMP)

I too was under the assumption that life had nothing to offer me, simply because I had nothing to offer life.

Not long ago, I traveled the path of the mundane, the mediocre. You know, the old "just barely getting by the skin of my teeth" road. Then one day, as I was running as fast as I could toward nowhere, I collided with the ugly truth—I was a wreck!

There are many degrees of disasters, and I could only compare my life thus far to a "clueless-ness" of a catastrophic nature.

Upon my awakening, I realized a great portion of my life had been spent in darkness and despair. Although I heartily subscribed to the belief that we all have a divine purpose and all possess a special gift, I began to believe I was somehow put out of the loop.

Apparently I am not alone. Many of us believe we missed the boat on happiness. Someway, somehow, despite God's infinite grace and love, we believe He deemed us "unacceptable" through some dastardly deed we committed.

God is not moody nor is He waiting for an opportunity to "get" you. God is ever-ready to come to our aid at any given moment. All we need do is ask.

As I set out on this mission to awaken the purpose God planted in my heart, I am learning the greatest weapon in conquering self-defeat rests in the simple question, "May I help you?"

My friend, if your hands are empty, hold someone else's. If you have nothing to give, give of your time and of yourself. If you are all alone, find someone who's lonely. If you are feeling sad, make someone happy.

The best gift you can give to yourself is to give your love to someone else.

The Lord promises us in His Word, "Give, and [gifts] will be given . . . For with the measure you deal out . . . it will be measured back to you (Luke 6:38 AMP). A promise is a promise. God promises His children life more abundant "till it overflows" (John 10:10 AMP).

What can you expect if you consciously, consistently open your life and heart to Jesus Christ? Over-the-top, overflowing living awaits you. You can count on it!

1
The Master of Mending

⧘⧘⧘

*D*ear God:

I am setting out on this mission with the faith that You will gird me with Your strength and encourage me with Your words. I cling to Your promise that You will not leave me nor forsake me. This journey is a path for me to bring healing to old wounds. As with all wounds, they must first be exposed, cleansed, and cared for before they can heal. This process can be painful, and I will need Your healing touch to carry me through. In the hope of discovering a new path for my life, I must reconstruct the old path.

It begins with the voice that echoed the same words again and again, "You are lazy, you're so slow, you are fat, you are stupid, you are ugly." It is not important where I first heard those words. That is not relevant to this healing process. The critical matter is how do I uproot these messages?

Each unkind word, when spoken, carries with it a dart that launches itself into the deep recesses of the mind; then eventually it becomes a part of the heart and soul. It drives itself deep enough to where I almost cannot find it. As it finds its resting spot, it carries a poison, one that seeps into my daily thought life. Every word I hear and speak becomes tainted and transformed by these distorted thought processes because I believed and accepted them as truth.

They make themselves at home as I reinforce negative thoughts by persistently accepting them.

Soon the work is done. The ray of hope I am born with, which inherently believes the best for me, becomes a spark. Eventually, hopes fade. As life disappoints, the light is extinguished. The lowly beast just leans back, relaxes, and watches while I unconsciously unleash the dragon with the same thoughts over and over. I learn to expect nothing good.

Before I know it, I begin to look to others to reinforce the pattern. I must be around those with whom I am comfortable. Sure I feel bad. But that is nothing new.

Feeling bad is normal for me. It is familiar. Why change?

Why? There is something deep down past the mind, past all human reasoning; the eternal heart beyond the human heart. It is the very conduit by which there is divine communication with God. It is the spirit. This is the inner voice sensing when something is wrong and alerting me of some offense against my person. If I have stilled the voice by consistently ignoring it, I condition myself to disregard my own spirit, my light of life force. Thus I begin to muffle my connection with peace and unity.

As I continue to engage in this downward spiral, any negative thoughts begin to feel intuitively true and factual. I dismiss any reasoning that this just doesn't make me feel good. I no longer trust feelings.

Experiences, instead of becoming a learning lesson, continue to disparage and degrade, only adding to the layers of decay stored in the mind. Unknowingly I continue to reject anything good or positive in my life simply because it just doesn't fit the mold. Would it have ever occurred to me that the mold was wrong from the start? Why not just break the mold and create a new one?

> And I am convinced and sure of this very thing,
> that He Who began a good work in you will
> continue until the day of Jesus Christ [right
> up to the time of His return], developing [that

good work] and perfecting and bringing it to full
completion in you. (Phil. 1:6 AMP)

Father:

I am not alone! Even though I know You're standing with me,
change sometimes hurts. Then I am reminded I am on Your potter's
wheel, and You know so much better than I what to do.

Lord, right now I am giving it all to You. I am placing in Your
hands the pain, the sorrow, all the memories from the yesterdays that
were buried deep within me. I am putting You in charge, knowing
You will never leave me or hurt me. I have Your promise, Your word
that I can always depend on You. In Jesus' name.

Personal Reflections

I need healing in:

_____

_____

_____

I need to recognize my truth was distorted by the following things I
heard being said to me. As a result, I believed a lie. List the thoughts
that were spoken to you and about you:

_____   _____

_____   _____

I need to speak forgiveness for the people who have hurt me. I must
make a conscious effort to ask God to help me to forgive. I list their
names below for all he, she, or they have done to me in my life.

_____

_____

_____

I also need to forgive myself for allowing people to hurt me. It is also important to take responsibility for the hurt by remembering we may have enabled others to hurt us. This does not apply to childhood abuse of any kind. Children are truly victims and are innocent. But even in these situations, we still need to forgive for our benefit.

Because of my past, I believed I was:

_____

_____

_____

Areas in which I previously felt weak or helpless because of my past:

_____

_____

_____

Areas where I believe I am now beginning to demonstrate strength are:

_____

_____

_____

2
Mourning into Joy

ear God:
In choosing the path to wholeness, I find myself dealing with emotions I had previously ignored. Sometimes bringing out what is hidden can feel so foreign and unsettling. As You help me to remember the hurt and pain I buried, my heart aches and feels heavy with sadness. While I am experiencing awareness of self, I lean on You at all times, Lord, and Your Word brings strength. With every angry, unkind word I recall, the dragon seemingly grows bigger. But it is only an illusion.

Just as we look in a microscope to see things closer, it only appears bigger. As I discover the real truth lies in uncovering the hurts and allowing You, Lord, in to heal the pain. Now I know the only illusion was keeping the pain hidden.

When I was a child, I was always told I was too sensitive. I remember feeling sadness to the point of tears, then I was ridiculed for being a cry baby. Soon the tears stopped and the sadness was buried deeper. Soon no one could see it, but I felt it. The sorrow echoed through the depths of my being.

Now I know I can have a gentle spirit and a tender heart for God. I can be strong, yet soft.

> Behold, I am sending you out like sheep in the
> midst of wolves; be wary and wise as serpents, and
> be innocent (harmless, guileless, and without falsity)
> as doves. (Matt. 10:16 AMP)

I am so strong in Your embrace, Lord. I rely on Your guidance to show me the way. I am now aware that human love is imperfect and fallible. I came to know that people usually live, behave, and think what they are taught. If they learn how to love a certain way, they will most likely display love in that particular fashion. Jesus even prayed to ask for forgiveness for the ones who treated Him horribly. "Father, forgive them, for they know not what they do" (Luke 23:34 AMP).

I was conditioned not to expect much of love. Why? I had grown to become disappointed in what life showed me of love.

All my life, I yearned for a love that felt blanket-soft and warm, welcoming. Instead, I received icy-cold, prickly sharp emotion that waits for a chance to jab and sting when my heart was exposed. The Psalms offered great comfort to me:

> Although my father and my mother have forsaken
> me, yet the Lord will take me up [adopt me as His
> child]. (Ps. 27:10 AMP)

In a sense, I gave up on love. How very glad I am, God, that You did not give up loving me. With Your strength, I will stave off all thoughts that this heart is beyond repair. I will not continue to be chiseled at until my heart is molded into something that no longer resembles a heart.

I am still me. But the best of me is yet to be. In a sense, I had buried myself beneath armor several layers thick. When I previously tried to shed the suit, I felt weary, overwhelmed with the task of bringing me to the surface. I will endeavor to reach that place where the dragon will not scorch me with his hot flames, as I bring my heart to the surface again. With You beside me, Lord, I will not fail.

Hurt wears anger and pride as a disguise for protection.

Am I angry with the person (or people) who has caused me pain? Dread would better describe the emotions I've felt. I dread that I have allowed myself the position where I exposed myself to such hurt. I dread having deep emotions. But I know that dread is fear, and You remind me, Lord, that we have not been given "a spirit of fear, but of power and of love and of a sound mind" (2 Tim. 1:7 NKJV).

In all my life, I believed that the feelings that were expressed to me were real love. But people will always fall short and disappoint because they are people. But now I know true love. Your love. That unconditional love You have for all opens our hearts, our minds, to expect all of the best from You. Now that I know this infinite love, I am not confined by limitations.

I am not a shallow pond. I am a wonderful, deep ocean. I thought I could be a pond, but I realize I was bound and restricted by burying my emotions. I must be what God created me to be and open those areas to experience true freedom.

I must turn to You, God, and turn everything over *to* You. Everything that this heart of mine has held and stored up through the years, I release to You with the confidence You will perfect that which concerns me.

Do I dare enter here
Where no one's been before?
Do you dread that life may stir
Where darkness guards the door?
If you do awaken the good that dwells in you,
You will not be forsaken,
Great beauty lies in truth.

And God's peace [shall be yours, that tranquil state of a soul assured of its salvation through Christ, and so fearing nothing from God and being content with its earthly lot of whatever sort that is, that peace] which transcends all understanding shall garrison and mount guard over your hearts and minds in Christ Jesus. (Phil. 4:7 AMP)

Lord:

Thank You for being my everything! You are my breath of life. You are my source of happiness and security. Never again do I have to question where I should turn, for You give me divine direction in all things. I thank You for always being there and being watchful over *all* my comings and goings. Please help me to remember You are always in control, and through You, I am whole. In Jesus' name.

Personal Reflections

My first step to bringing my heart out of its hiding place and closer to God is:

_____

_____

_____

I will lean on God, drawing from His love when I am feeling unloved by:

_____

_____

_____

I will ask God to help me deal with negative emotions (specify):

_____

_____

_____

I will employ His assistance with issues I previously found to be overwhelming, such as:

_____   _____

_____   _____

_____   _____

3

Breaking Tradition

*D*ear God:

Often times, we as human beings fall into the habit of tradition. We let tradition take over our thinking and invade our desire to change ourselves and our environment. We often reason in our minds, *This is the way it's always been.* We belabor the idea and walk in fear until we eventually cower and shrink back to our same, safe surroundings. We must learn to recognize that starting something new will feel uncomfortable and will work against our "inner grain." But, as we become more aware of our emotional senses, we'll allow and accept these feelings, not as normal (let us not use that term), but as part of our gradual metamorphosis into the wonderful persons God has created us to be.

Tradition was one of the reasons people would not acknowledge Jesus as Messiah even when He went about healing all who were sick and oppressed (Matt. 4:23). They refuted and denied Him because He was not following their traditions.

Jesus was a mold-breaker! The Pharisees and their kind lived by tradition. Every aspect of their life revolved around rituals and conformity to those rituals. Jesus' unique ways threatened and shook the very core of their religious doctrines. Jesus was a radical, and they were terrified of Him. He healed the sick on the Sabbath. He ate before performing the ceremonial washing of hands. He dined with tax collectors and women of questionable character. He even healed a blind man by putting His own sputum in his eyes. This was not their Messiah! The Messiah they *wanted* would not do these things. When Jesus road into town on a donkey, they were appalled by the very idea.

No Messiah of theirs would arrive by a donkey.

Jesus could see right through these men. Beneath all the adornments, the entrapments, the vestiges. He knew their hearts.

> But He said to them, Excellently and truly [so
> that there will be no room for blame] did Isaiah
> prophesy of you, the pretenders and hypocrites, as
> it stands written: These people [constantly] honor
> Me with their lips, but their hearts hold off and are
> far distant from Me. In vain (fruitlessly and without
> profit) do they worship Me, ordering and teaching
> [to be obeyed] as doctrines the commandments and
> precepts of men. You disregard and give up and ask
> to depart from you the commandment of God and
> cling to the tradition of men [keeping it carefully
> and faithfully]. And He said to them, You have a
> fine way of rejecting [thus thwarting and nullifying
> and doing away with] the commandment of God
> in order to keep your tradition (your own human
> regulations)! (Mark 7:6–9 AMP)

Living by tradition, and not the voice of God, these men missed the most precious gift to human existence—eternal life with God, our heavenly Father.

I also continue the cycle by being led not by the Spirit of God, but by my carnal mind and human reasoning. Scripture tells us, "For all who are led by the Spirit of God are sons of God" (Rom. 8:14 AMP).

We must constantly be in the process of renewing (restoring, repairing) our minds with the Word of God. This requires daily studying the Bible so we remain empowered by His strength, knowledge, and grace. The apostle Paul exhorted the Christians in Rome to do this very thing:

> Do not be conformed to this world (this age),
> [fashioned after and adapted to its external,
> superficial customs], but be transformed (changed)
> by the [entire] renewal of your mind [by its new
> ideals and its new attitude], so that you may prove
> [for yourselves] what is the good, and acceptable and
> perfect will of God, even the thing which is good
> and acceptable and perfect [in His sight for you].
> (Rom. 12:2 AMP)

When we conform to our traditional ways, we are not seeking God's greater good for our lives. God said, "Do not [earnestly] remember the former things; neither consider the things of old. Behold, I am doing a new thing!" (Isa. 43:18–19 AMP). He did not say, "Let everything remain as it is." "Sing to the Lord a new song, and His praise from the end of the earth!" (Isa. 42:10 AMP).

Conformity is just a fancy word for being a copycat!

Lord:

Help us to learn that change, although hard at times, can be a liberating, wonderful, knowledge-building, mind-expanding, learning experience that will only enhance our walk with You. If we really believe we should stay the same everyday, how can we believe that Your graces are new everyday? In Jesus' name.

Personal Reflections

The following are things I've previously done out of habit:

_____

_____

_____

Positive approaches to changes in these areas are:

_____

_____

_____

Emotions I am experiencing while renewing my mind are:

_____

_____

_____

4

Being Me—
The One God Sees

ear God:

   In seeking truth and liberty, I will continue on this journey of self-awareness. As I unearth the scars that had bound me, I will cling to Your peace and comfort. With every word I write, every page I turn, I ride on a wave of tranquility that rises with the tide of my emotions. I know I will experience times of sadness as I uncover what lies beneath the surface. But at those times, I will concentrate on my goal: To find the "me" underneath the tears, the years of rejection, resentment, sadness, and loneliness. It will not be too much for me to bear with You, God, at my side.

   Previously, when I experienced hurt, it created a smoke screen that disguised itself as feelings of inferiority, low self-esteem, unrealistic expectations of self, presumption (assuming the worst), and the list continues. When one weakness presented itself, it carried with it a host of other weaknesses that became my building blocks of self-defeat. In accepting continual negative reinforcement, the only service to me was in total ruination of my inner-value as a human being.

   Now I must wake up and become alert to what messages I send to myself.

I found an effective tool to be jotting down what I am thinking and becoming aware of how these thoughts affect my mood. In my experience, I have observed 99 percent of the time that my attitude becomes altered by some negative thought or notion I unconsciously impose upon myself or others.

In the aftermath of these thoughts, I become discouraged—and I'm not even aware of what discourages me. My freedom relies on identifying these thoughts and substituting them with positive ideas (God's Word). It is simply a matter of selective thinking. When I do something wrong, that does not mean I am stupid. The Bible says, I am of a "chosen generation, a royal priesthood, a holy nation" belonging to God (1 Pet. 2:9 NKJV). I am the King's daughter. I have a covenant, a divine inheritance. God's people "have the mind of Christ" (1 Cor. 2:16 NKJV). He will keep me in perfect peace when my mind is stayed upon Him (Isa. 26:3). These words, the true Word of God, when ingrained upon my heart, will establish a new, better foundation. Soon I will be hearing God's words echoing through my mind and heart, His own words of perfect excellence given exclusively to me as a gift to use everyday.

In retrospect, I now can see how believing the worst of myself and others had contaminated and distorted my thoughts, words, and actions. I had learned to view and process things through a very dark, indistinct mind's eye filter. In doing so, I had been creating my own personal purgatory. I felt sure of one thing: I was not in control. How very wrong feelings can sometimes be.

> Do not fret or have anxiety about anything, but in
> every circumstance and in everything, by prayer
> and petition (definite requests), with thanksgiving,
> continue to make your wants known to God. And
> God's peace [shall be yours, that tranquil state of a
> soul assured of its salvation through Christ, and so
> fearing nothing from God and being content with
> its earthly lot of whatever sort that is, that peace]
> which transcends all understanding shall garrison
> and mount guard over your hearts and minds in

Christ Jesus. For the rest, brethren, whatever is true,
whatever is worthy of reverence and is honorable
and seemly, whatever is just, whatever is pure,
whatever is lovely and lovable, whatever is kind and
winsome and gracious, if there is any virtue and
excellence, if there is anything worthy of praise,
think on and weigh and take account of these things
[fix your minds on them]. (Phil. 4:6–8 AMP)

Restore to me the joy of Your salvation and uphold
me with a willing spirit. (Ps. 51:12 AMP)

So Jesus said to those Jews who had believed in
Him, If you abide in My word [hold fast to My
teachings and live in accordance with them], you are
truly My disciples. And you will know the Truth,
and the Truth will set you free. (John 8:31–32 AMP)

I asked God
To tell you today,
He is transforming our lives
In miraculous ways.
He has healed all the wounds,
And now come the scars.
It is He who will soothe;
He's the mender of hearts.
He is bringing us into a time of change,
His love will help us to smile again.
I'm sorry the pain will sometimes bring hurt;
He is bringing our hearts to a place of rebirth.
I know this is hard to understand,
But know that we are part of God's plan.
Relying on Him, we will always be blessed.
God provides for His children, His personal best.

Father:

Help me to know that no matter what happens, I will always be Your child. As I learn to trust You more, I know You see all my fears. You will care for all my concerns, because that's just Who You are. You are always giving good things to Your children, and You always know what is best for me. Help me to continue to seek Your guidance every day. In Jesus' name.

Personal Reflections

The first thought of my day was:

_____

_____

_____

Something good I never realized about myself is:

_____

_____

_____

Are any negative thoughts consistently going through my mind?

_____

_____

_____

Did those thoughts cause a change in my attitude, emotions, or desires?

_____

_____

_____

How so?

_____

_____

_____

Healing thoughts for the day:

_____

_____

_____

_____

_____

5

The Reason for the Seasons

Dear God:

As I adjust to the changing of the seasons in the physical realm, I must also acclimate myself to change in my emotional and spiritual environment. Positive emotional and spiritual alterations require some time and effort to create worthwhile, lasting changes. I must tenaciously cling to the task set before me and decide that I am in this race to finish. Arming myself with the proper tools is essential as I tackle the dragons of the past and present.

My prayers should be seasoned with Bible verses on God's strength and endurance during these times of renewal.

> I have fought the good (worthy, honorable, and noble) fight, I have finished the race, I have kept (firmly held) the faith. (2 Tim. 4:7 AMP)

> [And indeed] the Lord will certainly deliver and draw me to Himself from every assault of evil. He will preserve and bring me safe unto His heavenly kingdom. (2 Tim. 4:18 AMP)

> For the Lord God helps Me; therefore have I not been ashamed or confounded. Therefore have I set

My face like a flint, and I know that I shall not be
put to shame. (Isa. 50:7 AMP)

At these times of refreshing, I must also build up my faith by
spending time in God's Word. This will empower me to overcome
any situation as it presents itself.

A good comparison would be a body builder in training. No
person beginning a weight training program starts with the heaviest
weights. This could result in an injury. When one begins, he should
start at a primary level, working at a steady pace until he reaches his
desired goal.

Likewise reshaping and reconditioning (renewing) my mind and
spirit must be approached one step at a time. Overall persistence is
the key to my succeeding. The Scriptures are God's building blocks
to strengthen me for these ongoing challenges. I must utilize His
Word to condition my mind and spirit. This is a battle. God's Word
and His Spirit are my sword.

Habitually writing down thoughts, I delve deeper and deeper into
my innermost being. One stroke of a pen at a time takes me closer to
the place where light will reveal all the past and present emotions I
had stored away in the darkness.

Clearing out my "emotional cobwebs," or cleaning house by
writing down my thoughts, can be one of the most effective strategies
to zero in on hidden offenses.

If some time goes by and I miss a few days (or weeks), that's OK.
I will just begin where I left off. The worst thing I can do is condemn
myself and give up.

**Everyone of us will make mistakes.
We are not perfect—just forgiven by His grace.**

Father:
Your light is glorious and there is no darkness in it. Sometimes
when I am in the dark, the light hurts until I adjust my eyes to it.
Through You, illumination always brings restoration, however. In
time, I will experience the fullness of Your radiance if I allow You

to bring me to that place. Strengthen me with Your love so I may be ready for the road of light ahead of me. In Jesus' name.

Personal Reflections

My favorite scripture is:

_____

_____

_____

Why?

_____

_____

_____

Areas on which I need to concentrate most:

_____

_____

_____

I see definite progress in:

_____

_____

_____

God has revealed to me that:

_____

_____

_____

Rays of light:

_____

_____

_____

Dark clouds:

_____

_____

_____

People I have found to be encouraging:

_____

_____

_____

6

Has Anyone Got a Light?

~~~~~~~

*D*ear God:

Many days had passed, and there seemed to be no break in the rain and darkness that settled over my window. All at once the sun burst through the clouds and shone into the room where I had been writing. As I glanced around the room, I noticed how dusty things appeared in the bright sunlight. When it was dark and gloomy, I could not see how badly the room needed to be cleaned. In my spirit, I heard these words: "Until you shed light on your circumstances, you are unable to see them clearly."

Lord, with Your light comes awareness. I am aware I must tend to the inside first, so I can effectively deal with my outside surroundings. Although my emotions cannot be seen in the physical sense, feelings shape the way I view my outward environment. Like the room, I must allow light to envelope my senses. Only then am I able to clear out the cobwebs in my mind and deal with unresolved issues.

I heard it said that if a mighty oak tree is in distress, it twists its inward parts to strengthen itself against further trauma. I too must look within and use what God has deposited in me to strengthen and build my inner man; thereby utilizing my God-given abilities to a greater extent.

Painful memories, like dust, will transform a shiny, new surface into a dull, worn-looking exterior unless I maintain awareness in myself. I must not focus on more than one emotion at a time, however, because the whole picture can be quite overwhelming to grasp. I realize that worthwhile, lifelong change begins one step at a time. I will stay true to my course and remain fixed on God to carry me through the rough patches. I bring all my emotions to the feet of Jesus to carry the burden for me.

Sadness, disappointment, depression, and hopelessness are related but have different levels of intensity. These emotions range from having a blue day to extreme periods of hopelessness and despair.

It is strictly up to me to determine if I can handle my feelings once I unearth them. Dealing with "the blues" is one thing, but a host of other emotional problems—which may be directly related to chemical, hormonal, or physical changes in the body—can complicate the situation.

It is up to me to use my good judgment and look beyond myself for support when it is needed. Sometimes it is necessary to seek counseling, or to speak to a pastor trained in counseling, to work through issues.

It may take some time to get connected with the right resources, but I will be persistent and I will not fear. I am a child of the King, which entitles me to special privileges. I will always keep in mind that God wants me to have the very best, and I should not settle for anything less than I deserve. He wants His children blessed.

Rely on His rest; Father knows best.

I have strength for all things in Christ Who empowers me [I am ready for anything and equal to anything through Him Who infuses inner strength into me; I am self-sufficient in Christ's sufficiency]. (Phil. 4:13 AMP)

For God did not give us a spirit of timidity (of cowardice, of craven and cringing and fawning fear), but [He has given us a spirit] of power and of love

and of calm and well-balanced mind and discipline
and self-control. (2 Tim. 1:7 AMP)

But let all those who take refuge and put their trust
in You rejoice; let them ever sing and shout for
joy, because You make a covering over them and
defend them; let those also who love Your name be
joyful in You and be in high spirits. For You, Lord,
will bless the [uncompromisingly] righteous [him
who is upright and in right standing with You]; as
with a shield You will surround him with goodwill
(pleasure and favor). (Ps. 5:11–12 AMP)

But the wisdom from above is first of all pure
(undefiled); then it is peace-loving, courteous
(considerate, gentle). [It is willing to] yield to
reason, full of compassion and good fruits; it
is wholehearted and straightforward, impartial
and unfeigned (free from doubts, wavering, and
insincerity). And the harvest of righteousness (of
conformity to God's will in thought and deed)
is [the fruit of the seed] sown in peace by those
who work for and make peace [in themselves
and in others, that peace which means concord,
agreement, and harmony between individuals, with
undisturbedness, in a peaceful mind free from fears
and agitating passions and moral conflicts. (James
3:17–18 AMP)

And my God will liberally supply (fill to the full)
your every need according to His riches in glory in
Christ Jesus. (Phil. 4:19 AMP)

*D*ear Lord:
        As You have given Your children a free will and a choice
for our lives, I now choose peace. I no longer want to be enslaved

by memories of the past. I ask You to help me remove the chains and help bring me into a new day of restoration and freedom. I am confident You will supply *all* my needs for You are Jehovah-Jireh, the Lord, our provider. In Jesus' name.

Personal Reflections

I realize I tend to feel hurt when:

_____

_____

_____

Memories I find to be painful:

_____

_____

_____

The ways God and I are resolving inner conflicts:

_____

_____

_____

I feel optimistic about:

_____

_____

_____

The best thing about being "me" is:

_____

_____

_____

7
No Wrong Turns

❦

*D*ear God:

Driving to a friend's house one day, I realized I knew only one way to get to her street. But as it turned out, it was not the right way. I suddenly thought of my friend, and it occurred to me how many routes she would know after having lived there for many years. It was then, Lord, You brought to my mind about preparing, being equipped in this life. If I had asked for an alternate way, I would not be lost at this point.

Sometimes it's that way with Your children, Lord. The Bible contains all of the answers to life's questions, if I only knew Your Word. The better I know Your Word, the more equipped I am to deal with the struggles of life. Writing the Word on the tablets of my heart, ingraining it into my spirit, will prepare me for any storm that comes along. Utilizing the Scriptures will direct my paths toward the ultimate route for me. There will be no dead ends, no wrong turns. I will never lose my way with You as my navigator.

The more scriptures I know, the more doors I can open to total restoration and freedom. In essence, what I don't know will hurt me.

If I continually drove my car around the same block, I would soon grow weary. The same applies when I am faced with an issue and I have no idea how to solve it. Soon I feel lost in my circumstances, and there seems to be no way out.

Praying regularly and reading and applying God's Word will transport me from a dead-end road to my victorious, God-given destination.

> And your ancient ruins shall be rebuilt; you shall raise up the foundations of [buildings that have laid waste for] many generations; and you shall be called Repairer of the Breach, Restorer of Streets to Dwell In. (Isa. 58:12 AMP)

> So Jesus said to those Jews who had believed in Him, If you abide in My word [hold fast to My teachings and live in accordance with them], you are truly My disciples. And you will know the Truth, and the Truth will set you free. (John 8:31–32 AMP)

> As for God, His way is perfect; the word of the Lord is tried. He is a Shield to all those who trust and take refuge in Him. (2 Sam. 22:31 AMP)

Father:

Thank You for giving me Your Word to light my way through the darkness. I am so blessed to have Your Holy Spirit to whisper words of Your hope, love, and guidance.

As I travel through every situation in life, remind me to arm myself by renewing my mind with Your Word everyday. In Jesus' name.

Personal Reflections

Situations in which I previously felt lost:

_____

_____

_____

I trust God for (promises):

_____

_____

_____

I rely and depend on God for:

_____

_____

_____

The best time for me to study and pray is:

_____

_____

_____

Why?

_____

_____

_____

8

The Past is in the Past—At Last!

❦

*D*ear God:

One of the most important ways of renewing my mind is coming to terms with the past and freeing myself. By making peace with that which robs me of my joy, I will be well on my way to total liberation from my thought life.

Being human, I am subject to shortcomings, and I find my life is checkered with many situations I now view as painful. Children of dysfunctional families often feel helpless about what we can do to change surroundings. I may have realized early on (based on my perceptions) that my environment was far from ideal. Whether I was aware of it then or did not recognize it until later, I could do nothing to alter my past; but with God, I *can* transform my future.

In redefining myself, I must be determined to purge my mind of the pain by acknowledging it and forgiving those who inflicted this pain. This presents a challenge as I may tend to hold on to pain, feeling justified because perhaps I was the victim of past injustices. Whether inflicted intentionally or unintentionally, the pain is still the same. Pain is pain. It scars, it wounds, it festers at the core of my very being. The ultimate tragedy is the pain continues to infect and inflict me as long as I hold onto it.

Growing seeds of sadness and hatred within only serves to close the door on blessings and joy in my life. If I recognize the memory as a poison invading my body, continuing to rob me of life's very essence, it is likely I will want to end this destructive cycle.

Forgiving and letting go do not absolve the offending party or parties. They are not off the hook. I am. I must remember that God is my vindicator.

I learned that being right or feeling justified over a wrong suffered does not help me to sleep better at night. Being at peace with God and others does, however.

One day, while talking to my mother on the phone, we exchanged words. My mother ended the argument by hanging up on me. I saw no justifiable reason for her behavior.

Well, I thought, *I won't be calling her back.*

God replied inside me, *Oh, yes you will.*

"But God, I'm right about this!" I said assuredly.

Do you want to be right, or do you want to follow Me?

Ouch! I could have held on to my anger and let it make a home in my heart. But I didn't. I knew holding onto it would only breed more anger. So I called my mom.

"Let's not fight," I said. "Life is too short to stay angry with each other."

It is not important to call everyone in my life to resolve past differences. The importance lies in making peace within. God will take care of the rest for me.

> If possible, as far as it depends on you, live at peace
> with everyone. Beloved, never avenge yourselves,
> but leave the way open for [God's] wrath; for it is
> written, Vengeance is Mine, I will repay (requite),
> says the Lord. (Rom. 12:18–19 AMP)

> Be gentle and forbearing with one another and,
> if one has a difference (a grievance or complaint)
> against another, readily pardoning each other; even

as the Lord has [freely] forgiven you, so must you
also [forgive]. (Col. 3:13 AMP)

Father:

Help me to understand that holding grudges or hurts against
another only serves to grow roots of bitterness, anger, and hatred,
thereby causing decay to spread in my heart. Its sole function is to
enable the enemy to gain ground, which will only hinder my walk
with You. Help me to see I am the one who reaps the bitter fruits of
the bitter seeds I sow. Deliver me from "heart decay" for all time by
helping me to get a revelation that Your love conquers all and Your
grace is sufficient for forgiving anything in my past, present, and
future. In Jesus' name.

Personal Reflections

Through God, I believe I am being set free from:

_____

_____

_____

Recent attitude adjustments I have made in my life:

_____

_____

_____

I am learning to be flexible in areas of:

_____

_____

_____

I quickly forgave _____ for what (he/she/they) did
to me recently. I showed it by:

_____

_____

_____

9

I Am Forgiven—Forever

***

*D*ear God:

    I think one of the most difficult things to overcome, more than forgiving others, is forgiving myself. I am much more critical of my mistakes than I am of another's. I beat, condemn, and persecute myself far beyond what I would allow another (no matter how evil he is) to be punished.

Self-condemnation takes on many disguises and ruthlessly plucks the life out of someone who is under its power. Guilt, insecurity, low self-esteem, lack of interest or desire for better in life, complacency, depression, and self-pity are just a few masks self-hatred wears to keep me stuck and prevent me from experiencing any growth in my life.

All these emotions render me powerless to make any positive changes, and I then resort to a mindset that I am incapable of altering my thinking, thus creating an "emotional paralysis" of my own design. I become a prisoner of my own "stinking thinking" by concluding, "I think. I feel. Therefore, I am and I will always be." Rubbish! The devil is the accuser of the brethren (Rev.12:10). He roams the earth like a roaring lion seeking whom he should devour (1 Pet. 5:8). Am I going to allow the devil to feast on me, making a meal of my mind all my life?

While I consciously choose to forgive myself, I will also engrain these powerful words into my mind: I am the righteousness of God in and through Christ (2 Cor. 5:21). I am of a chosen race, a royal priesthood, of God's own purchased, special people. He has called me out of darkness into His marvelous light (1 Peter 2:9).

Jesus said, "I am the Way and the Truth and the Life" (John 14:6 AMP). If I am to obtain forgiveness and peace for myself, it is only through Jesus Christ. Jesus speaks of this true peace as "not as the world gives" (John 14:27 AMP), but accessible only through the Father, Son, and Holy Spirit. God's peace is obtainable—all I need do is ask. "Ask, and keep on asking and you will receive, so that your joy (gladness, delight) may be full and complete" (John 16:24 AMP).

God does not play favorites! He is "no respecter of persons" (Acts 10:34 AMP). "You do not have, because you do not ask" (James 4:2 AMP).

Countless Bible verses contain the one power-filled word that connects me to God's miracles. *Ask.* This is the common thread to all the great works of the Bible. Every scripture that includes receiving from God also involves asking.

When I am reluctant to ask for something, it is usually because I am afraid of rejection. God promises, "I will never leave you nor forsake you" (Heb. 13:5 NKJV).

God's Word commands me to "come boldly to the throne of grace, that we may obtain mercy and find grace to help in time of need" (Heb. 4:16 NKJV).

Father:

I thank You all Your promises are "yes and amen." All I need do is open my mouth and ask. You will give me anything in accordance with Your will. It may not be when or how I want it, but it is always the perfect time because You are never late.

Lord, help me to know that delay does not mean denial. Abraham waited for many years for His promise to be fulfilled, and yet he staggered not at Your promises. He never wavered in his faith (Rom. 4:20).

Help me to renew my mind in Your Word. Remove any doubt from my mind and continue to infuse me with Your wondrous strength. I will prayerfully persist until You positively provide the promise. I ask all things in Jesus' name. Amen.

True faith is not only the belief that God will answer all prayers but the assurance of His knowing all our needs before we even ask.

Personal Reflections

Something new I am believing God for:

_____

_____

_____

I am finally forgiving myself for:

_____

_____

_____

Being critical of my_____
has been a challenge in the past.

God will forgive me because:

_____

_____

_____

10
The Power of the Tongue

Dear God:

On the road to total restoration and wholeness, I will seek to gather the pieces of myself that had been lost along the way. Life is a journey, not a destination, and through negative experiences, I may tend to feel I have lost a piece of myself—my heart, my self-esteem, my joy —along the way. Memories, like pieces of a great puzzle, will create a complete picture of my whole being if I gather them up, sort them out, and put them in the proper order. My aim is to gain a clearer perspective and insight into my past, in order to make peace inside myself. It is possible to obtain through God a sense of wholeness (well-being and peace) within myself and with my world.

Another step in the progression to completion takes me to a place where I need to make major changes: My confessions—simply put, my mouth, my tongue.

> Death and life are in the power of the tongue, and they who indulge in it shall eat the fruit of it [for death or life]. (Prov. 18:21 AMP)

> He who guards his mouth and his tongue keeps himself from troubles. (Prov. 21:23 AMP)

{39}

> Pleasant words are as a honeycomb, sweet to the
> mind and healing to the body. (Prov. 16:24 AMP)

> Likewise, look at the ships: though they are so great
> and are driven by rough winds, they are steered by
> a very small rudder wherever the impulse of the
> helmsman determines. Even so the tongue is a little
> member, and it can boast of great things. See how
> much wood or how great a forest a tiny spark can
> set ablaze. And the tongue is a fire. [The tongue
> is a] world of wickedness set among our members,
> contaminating and depraving the whole body and
> setting on fire the wheel of birth (the cycle of man's
> nature), being itself ignited by hell (Gehenna).
> (James 3:4–6 AMP)

Words, once spoken, are mighty containers of power. I can (by my words) choose prosperity, health, and happiness for my life or live a life of poverty, sickness, and despair. This is not debatable; it is God's law.

> For out of the fullness (the overflow, the
> superabundance) of the heart the mouth speaks.
> (Matt. 12:34 AMP)

> There is not [even] one thing outside a man which
> by going into him can pollute and defile him; but
> the things which come out of a man are what defile
> him and make him unhallowed and unclean. (Mark
> 7:15 AMP)

What I may believe to be harmless words will, in fact, set the stage for success or failure in my life. One word at a time, one sentence at a time, one day at a time, I mold my future. Before God's Word shed light on this subject, I never realized the potential, the power, and the ability I possessed to alter my existence.

Here is an exercise I tried. For just one day, I was completely aware of every word I spoke or thought of speaking. If I said something negative, I wrote it down. At the end of the day, I counted how many negative words I spoke. Then I wrote beside each one a positive statement I could have used in its place. I started incorporating positive confessions until it became a habit for me—a life-changing habit I did not want to break.

Unspoken

It appears as though my world has caved in, broken at the seams,
The picture of my life looks grim. What will this day bring?
My flesh just cannot comprehend how God could fix this mess.
I will not let my mouth confess, no cursed words leave these lips.
God has said, in His own Book, the words we speak are power.
When the words we speak are negative, we turn our good fruit sour.
Our daily life confessions should line up with His Word.
Our God will take possession if we speak the words that serve.
No matter how things look to us, we must not confess doubt.
It's time to pray, to praise, and trust. Don't let those bad thoughts out.
A negative word unspoken is a thought that is not birthed.
The seed of doubt is broken; we wreck the devil's curse.
Our hope and joy are in the Lord. We are strengthened by His blood.
We're blessed, we're loved, we're rich, we're healed. How gracious is our God!
Shout it from the mountaintops. He'll rise to meet your faith,
And suddenly (it won't be long), all circumstances change.

Below are a list of some of the negative statements spoken consciously and unconsciously:
I'm exhausted (tired).

I feel like death warmed over.
I'm always broke.
He'll never change.
I can't do anything right.
My kids never listen.
I'm always hungry.
I'm so stupid.
You never listen to me.
I can't.
He'll never amount to anything.
I was never good at managing money.
I have a short temper.
You're so slow.
I can't think straight.
We never have enough money.
We'll always be in debt.
There's not enough hours in the day.
I'm losing my mind.
Be careful (full of care).
He's so bad.
You make me sick.
You're such a loser.
You're going to fall and break your neck.

Once I realized all the negative words I used, I wondered why I never questioned these words before.

At first I reasoned, "It's just an expression. It doesn't mean anything." That is just what the enemy wants me to think. The devil is the master of deception. If I am not wise to his tactics, I will fall victim to his traps every time I speak.

Being a child of the King should shine through in every area of my life. Speaking words of victory, not defeat, helps me to assume my place as a joint heir of the kingdom.

Just as exercise is good for the body, I must also take authority over my mouth. The tongue is (and forever will be) unruly and carnal because my mind is also. Therefore, I must bring it into submission by continually "renewing" it with the Word.

If I continually speak negative and sinful words, I will live by those same words.

I must also reflect on what I feed my mind. If my thoughts are negative and impure, perhaps it is because I plant those things into my mind with everything I see and hear. The television programs I watch, the music I listen to, the people I associate with, and the books I read are directly responsible for the good or bad fruit in my life. I must remember what I sow, I will eventually reap.

I will start proclaiming the positive, and I will watch God work! What I say and see (envision), I will be.

It is not enough for me to stop saying negative words. I must also replace those thoughts and words with positive thoughts and words. In doing so, I will reap a tremendous harvest in my life.

Below is my list of positive confessions, taken from God's Word, to think and say over my life everyday.

I am blessed and not cursed (Deut. 23:5)

I have peace. (Phil. 4:7)

I am the righteousness of God through Christ (2 Cor. 5:21)

God will supply my every need. (Phil. 4:19)

By Jesus' stripes, I am healed (Isa. 53:5)

Everything I put my hand to, prospers. (3 John 2)

I am useful, helpful, kind, understanding, and forgiving. (Eph. 4:32)

I am a doer of God's Word. (James 1:22)

I am patient in waiting for what God has for me. (Rom. 8:25)

God's grace is sufficient for me. (2 Cor. 12:9)

With God in my life, all things are possible. (Mark 10:27)

I am not afraid! (Heb. 13:6)

I trust in the Lord with all my heart. (Ps. 62:8)

I give thanks to God for *all* things. (1 Thess 5:18)

I have more than enough. (2 Cor. 9:10–11)

He gives me wisdom. (James 1:5)

He fills me with joy. (Rom. 15:13)

Father:

I thank You for teaching me to speak words of life. I confess everyday, in everyway, I will yield to Your Spirit and speak words that infuse me with power, strength, and love. It's so wonderful to know You are concerned with all my needs before I even know them. In Jesus' name.

Personal Reflections

Some negative statements I have made:

_____

_____

_____

_____

I will rephrase those statements:

_____

_____

_____

_____

Things I have heard others say:

_____

_____

_____

Today is going to be a good day because:

_____

_____

_____

Everyday I feel more:

_____

_____

_____

11

Forgive and Forget— For Good!

~~~~~~~~~~~~~~

*D*ear God:

    As I walk Your way and do Your will for my life, You allow challenges to come to test my strength in You. I encounter people who seem judgmental and condemning. They do not understand the walk, the path on which You lead me. You challenge me by repeating the same words Jesus spoke as they were condemning, beating, and killing Him. "Forgive them." I *will* myself to forgive them, Lord. I will not let anyone or anything have priority over You and Your will for my life.

    I hear Your voice echo, "Care not." That is not to say I do not care about them, but rather I *cannot* care. I choose not to allow angry or cutting words to come inside and cause hurt. I realize that I can't make everyone like and approve of me. I must care more about impressing God than I do about impressing others. I choose to love people with the same love You bestow upon all Your children—*agape* (unconditional) love.

    Being human, I am subject to shortcomings and human reasoning. You help me to know they too are walking the walk, and judging them is no different than them judging me. It makes no difference if my cause for anger and hurt is justifiable. Vengeance is Yours, Lord, and I should have no place for revenge in my heart.

> But He said to me, My grace (My favor and loving-kindness and mercy) is enough for you [sufficient against any danger and enables you to bear the trouble manfully]; for My strength and power are made perfect (fulfilled and completed) and show themselves most effective in [your] weakness. (2 Cor. 12:9 AMP)

Therefore, I care not what men think or say about me. I only care to impress You, God.

Feelings concerning past injustices done only breed contempt and bitterness. I will not entertain emotions of a negative or scornful nature. I will not be offended; I will not seek vengeance. I will look for the good in people, and I want the very best for them that God has to offer.

These are Your ways, Lord. I consciously choose to walk in Your light and abide in it.

There is no darkness in light, so I must cast aside all thoughts, reasonings, and impressions that try to steal my place in the light. I no longer dwell in dark shadows of the past, but I stand secured in the spotlight of Your love and grace where I know I am safe.

Lord:

Everyday I consciously choose to reflect over the previous day. I ask Your help in reminding me of anytime I was offended or was offensive toward others. I am confident that as soon as I lay this issue before You, I am forgiven. It is like holding on to a helium balloon. Once I let go, it is forever gone. In forgiving, I realize I must also forget the offense. If I do not forget, I cannot truly forgive. I thank You, Father, for teaching me how to be free! In Jesus' name.

Personal Reflections

Some ways I had felt condemnation were:

_____
_____
_____

I am working to resolve this by:

_____
_____
_____

I have become more verbal about:

_____
_____
_____

I consciously forgive and forget (with God's help) a situation I have held onto for a long time because:

_____
_____
_____

How did I handle the situation after I gave it to God?

_____
_____
_____

A new way to resolve hurt in my life is:

_____
_____
_____

12

Where is Your Wilderness?

Dear God:
   I have found this scripture to be a continual source of inspiration in troubled times.

> For the Lord will comfort Zion; He will comfort all
> her waste places. And He will make her wilderness
> like Eden, and her desert like the garden of the
> Lord. Joy and gladness will be found in her,
> thanksgiving and the voice of song or instrument of
> praise. (Isa. 51:3 AMP)

During this time of renewal and change, God asks me: Where is your wilderness?

It is essential that I recognize the primary purpose for God bringing me into the wilderness. There, by putting aside all confusion and calamity, I can quiet my mind to hear His voice—His still, small voice.

> Let be and be still, and know (recognize and
> understand) that I am God. (Ps. 46:10 AMP)

The first four letters in the word restoration is R-E-S-T. Yes, Lord, with Your blessing comes resting. Resting in Your love, Your peace, Your Word. Resting does not mean worrying, fretting, or being anxious about issues I have no control over. God's Word states:

> Strengthen (complete, perfect) and make you what
> you ought to be and equip you with everything good
> that you may carry out His will. (Heb. 13:21 AMP)

Therefore, I must consciously make a decision to cast all my cares upon Him.

> Casting the whole of your care [all your anxieties,
> all your worries, all your concerns, once and for all]
> on Him, for He cares for you affectionately and
> cares about you watchfully. (1 Pet. 5:7 AMP)

At these times of reflection, I must be careful not to entertain thoughts not of God.

> Brethren, do not be children [immature] in your
> thinking; continue to be babes in [matters of]
> evil, but in your minds be mature [men]. (1 Cor.
> 14:20 AMP)

I must seize the opportunity and use the time to bring me closer to God and seek to gain insight into His wisdom and knowledge.

In the secret, quiet place, the distracting elements of life are stilled by the serenity of being one with God. In that time, I can think clearly, pray clearly, and listen clearly to His message spoken exclusively for me. He speaks softly the ministering words of love to His precious children. He knows exactly what I need to hear in order to help me to grow in Him. He knows my heart. He can read my thoughts. He can see all my tomorrows before they occur. He knows my beginning from my end.

Once I get a revelation of His glory, the awesome power God has, I am never the same again. A small glimpse into His goodness will cast radiant light on any dismal situation, no matter how dark it appears. All I need do is get alone with God.

Where is my wilderness? The answer lies inside. I can create one solitary place in the midst of my being where no one else can go. It's reserved for only God and me.

Personal Reflections

Where is my wilderness?

_____

_____

_____

How often do I take time to be with God?

_____

_____

_____

Should I take more time to be alone with God?_____ If I did, how would I spend that additional time?

_____

_____

_____

Do I think of *time* as a thief or a gift?

_____

_____

Has my opinion recently changed?_____ Why or why not?

_____

_____

_____

13

Don't Let Your Solitary Be Sedentary

ear God:
It has been said, "Time waits for no man." This is true. I must become more aware of this fact and use my time wisely.

When an opportunity presents itself, I should seize the moment and utilize it to the best of my ability. Often, when my time is freed up, I tend to waste it by dwelling on negative thoughts. I fill my space with waste, and the tragedy is I can never get time back once I use it. When my children were small, I remember wishing I had more time to myself. I wasted time dwelling on the fact that I had no time, thereby continuing the cycle of throwing my time away. As my children got older, I had more time to spend by myself. Was I a good steward of that time? Not really. It seemed the more free time I had, the better I got at wasting it.

I have recently become more aware of my time, and I consciously work not to waste it by watching television (unless there is a program that's beneficial to my spiritual growth) or listening to music (with the exception of praise and worship music). I continually weigh my activities by asking: Will this activity bear good or bad fruit (or nothing) in my life? I must no longer allow time to be a robber but a gift to me.

> And who knows but that you have come to the
> kingdom for such a time as this and for this very
> occasion? (Esther 4:14 AMP)

> Lord, make me to know my end and [to appreciate]
> the measure of my days—what it is; let me know
> and realize how frail I am [how transient is my stay
> here]. (Ps. 39:4 AMP)

I will let time run its steady course. I will revel in the knowledge
my days on this earth were well spent, seasoned with the grace,
knowledge, and riches only God can provide for me.

> O [earnestly] remember how short my *time* is and
> what a mere fleeting life mine is. (Ps. 89:47 AMP)

God will give me the most for my moments if I devote my time
to Him. He is the greatest teacher, and He will utilize my time to
the fullest extent. As I grow in the knowledge of His Word, I will
witness firsthand how He brings His Word to life throughout my
daily living. He will walk me through my ups and downs and build
my character along the way.

> For I have learned how to be content (satisfied to
> the point where I am not disturbed or disquieted) in
> whatever state I am. I know how to be abased and
> live humbly in straitened circumstances, and I know
> also how to enjoy plenty and live in abundance. I
> have learned in any and all circumstances the secret
> of facing every situation, whether well-fed or going
> hungry, having a sufficiency and enough to spare or
> going without and being in want. I have strength
> for all things in Christ Who empowers me [I am
> ready for anything and equal to anything through
> Him Who infuses inner strength into me; I am self-
> sufficient in Christ's sufficiency]. (Phil. 4:11–13 AMP)

Lord, in areas where I had exhibited weaknesses, You will strengthen me. You will build me up, empower me, through Your Spirit and Your Word. You will season me through difficulties by causing me to lean totally on You. You will reveal to me areas that need to be dealt with and work with me continually until I am where You want me to be. In Jesus' name.

> And I am convinced and sure of this very thing,
> that He Who began a good work in you will
> continue until the day of Jesus Christ [right
> up to the time of His return], developing [that
> good work] and perfecting and bringing it to full
> completion in you. (Phil. 1:6 AMP)

Personal Reflections

With God's help, I will try to use my time in a more constructive way by:

_____

_____

_____

Time robbers of the past (old attitude):

_____

_____

_____

Time gifts for the future (new attitude):

_____

_____

_____

14

Be Assured, My Word is True

ear God:

Today I was praying and suddenly a thought came into my mind. *How do you know His Word is true?* Of course, I recognized this thought was not of You.

I was pouring water from a pitcher at the time, and I heard You say, "As certain as you know that water will pour *down* into this glass, you should be assured My Word will come to pass!"

Suddenly I thought of the water pouring and realized how I take this for granted. If it were not for gravity, I could not even pour water into a glass. Without gravity, it would go up. But, because this has been tested and tried, I think nothing of it.

Regardless of the advances of modern technology, gravity remains a wonder of science. Yet who created gravity? How can I have faith in the invention and not have faith in the inventor?

> As for God, His way is perfect! The word of the
> Lord is tested and tried; He is a shield to all those
> who take refuge and put their trust in Him. (Ps.
> 18:30 AMP)

Every word of God is tried and purified. (Prov. 30:5
AMP)

The grass withers, the flowers fades, but the word of
our God will stand forever. (Isa. 40:8 AMP)

For in Him we live and move and have our being.
(Acts 17:28 AMP)

God placed the stars in the sky and sustains them by His mighty
hand. He synchronized the orbit of the planets and maintains their
placement in the heavens. Yet He manages to stay and dwell in me.
He concerns Himself with all my needs as well. He even knows the
number of hairs on my head. He knows all my sins and yet He still
loves me. How is this possible? I realized His awesome power and
His tremendous love for me were beyond my comprehension. His
awesome power and His tremendous love for all are inconceivable to
the human mind. I must remember, He is God.

When I view and consider Your heavens, the work
of Your fingers, the moon and the stars, which You
have ordained and established, what is man that
You are mindful of him, and the son of [earthborn]
man that You care for him? Yet You have made
him but a little lower than God [or heavenly
beings], and You have crowned him with glory and
honor. (Ps. 8:3–5 AMP)

For the Lord is good; His mercy and loving-
kindness are everlasting, His faithfulness and truth
endure to all generations. (Ps. 100:5 AMP)

I shudder and wince in fear for people who make comments such
as "God didn't write the Bible; men wrote it," or "That was written
for those times; it's different now." If only they could see that God's
Word is for yesterday, today, and forever. But their eyes are blinded

by sin, and they do not even realize that they are lost and doomed without His saving grace, His eternal love, His Son. I pray Ephesians 1:17–20 and 3:16–19 to intercede for the people I know who are lost, and I am seeing positive changes in their lives. God's Word is true!

Father:

My delight is to do Your will, O God, and my desire is to fulfill Your purpose on this earth. I cleave to Your mercy and submit myself to serve You. I commission to walk the way of the light. I will cling to You and will bind truth and mercy about my neck. I will gird my loins with Your Spirit and let Your love continually abide in me.

I will wear wisdom as a compass and wage war against all attempts to capture my joy.

You are the One who seasons me for the battle. You strengthen my inner being. Your voice speaks to me in tender whispers. I listen and obey.

Although I am not always obedient, You wait patiently until I see the error of my ways. Soon I call out to You. You welcome me with open arms. Your love invites me in.

You are my Abba Father, my breath of life within. In Jesus' name.

Personal Reflections

God says, "I know the thoughts and plans I have for you, . . . for welfare and peace . . . , to give you hope in your final outcome." (Jer. 29:11 AMP) What do I think is God's plan for me?

_____

_____

_____

_____

_____

Have my plans been altered by a recent awareness of myself or an awareness of God's love for me? _____Why?

_____

_____

_____

Has forgiveness and healing of myself toward self, God, or others played a role in defining where I will go in life? _____Why?

_____

_____

_____

15

Don't Just Think It— Speak It and Seek It

❧⟨───✦⟨❈⟩✦───⟩❧

D ear God:
     The biggest challenge thus far has been consistently speaking Your Word during life's challenges. I have learned not to speak the negative, but now I must focus on speaking the positive, God-given Word over my life.

> But the word is very near you, in your mouth and in
> your mind and in your heart, so that you can do it.
> (Deut. 30:14 AMP)

God, I must train my thoughts to agree with Your will and Your thoughts. The first place to start is to begin speaking positive scriptures over and into my life. If I start to doubt, I cast doubt out. I proclaim Your Word. No matter what the circumstances look like, I continue to be obedient to You, God.

> And be constantly renewed in the spirit of your
> mind [having a fresh mental and spiritual attitude],
> and put on the new nature (the regenerate

self) created in God's image, [Godlike] in true
righteousness and holiness. (Eph. 4:23–24 AMP)

Being renewed in my mind means to daily cast down *every*
thought that exalts itself against the true knowledge of God's Word
(2 Cor. 10:5) and be constantly (always) aware of the words that I
speak. I will constantly let my life lovingly express truth in all things,
through words and deeds (Eph. 4:15).

Minds are carnal and are subject to human thoughts, reasonings,
and motives (Rom. 8:6–7). Without the Holy Spirit to help me
everyday, I am helpless against the attacks of the enemy (Rom. 8:26–
27).

When I enlist the help of the Holy Spirit, I exchange my
weaknesses for God's strength, my words for God's Word, my
wickedness for God's love. If I yield to His gentle voice, to His ever-
so-soft tugging, I will become a living example of God. The secret
lies in continual submission to Him.

With God's Spirit inside me, He will make me aware of a
potentially sinful situation before it happens. I may have an angry
thought and want to speak angry words. The Bible tells us, "When
angry, do not sin." (Eph. 4:26 AMP) It does not say *not* to feel anger.
When we speak in haste, we only say hurtful and malicious things.
The Bible says, "I will take heed and guard my ways, that I may sin
not with my tongue; I will *muzzle* my mouth as with a bridle while
the wicked are before me" (Ps. 39:1 AMP).

Yes, even while the wicked are before me, I must hold my
tongue.

Anger is a human emotion, and it takes a great deal of restraint
to hold it back. Jesus felt anger, but He did not allow His anger to
cause Him to sin. He relied on the Holy Spirit to help Him choose
words that reflected God's love.

Relying on the Holy Spirit, I too can choose words of life—not
death. Instead of saying, "I am so mad at you right now. I hate you.
You make me sick." I should say, "We need to discuss what's just
happened. I feel hurt by what you just said (did)."

God has not called me to be a doormat. He does not want me to be walked on or taken advantage of by others. There are ways of expressing my emotions without inflicting hurt on others. Doing so only causes bitterness to grow in my heart. Bitter seeds grow bitter fruit.

The key, I have found, is to think before I speak. "Am I going to resolve this problem by verbally attacking this person?" All signs point to no. When I sow (say) words of anger, anger is what I reap (receive). No matter what, God's Word is true in *all things*.

"For whatever a man sows, that he will also reap" (Gal. 6:7 NKJV). I will get my point across. I will get it off my chest. But before I do, I will ask the Holy Spirit to guide me. He will not steer me wrong. I will sow love, and love is what *I* will reap.

> But I say, walk and live [habitually] in the [Holy] Spirit [responsive to and controlled and guided by the Spirit]; then you will *certainly* not gratify the cravings and desires of the flesh (of human nature *without God*). (Gal. 5:16 AMP)

God's Word says, "Let your speech always be with grace, seasoned with salt, that you may know how you ought to answer each one" (Col. 4:6 NKJV). I thought about that for awhile and realized that it takes time to add seasoning to food. But if I add something (like salt), it always makes food taste better. The same should apply to my words. I should think before I speak. Just as I do not want to add too much salt to any food, I should not talk too much, or talk just to fill in the conversation. Jesus said, "Let your Yes be simply Yes, and your No be simply No" (Matt. 5:37 AMP), meaning I should say what I mean and mean what I say. As a child of the King, I do not want a reputation for prattling on, which can then lead to gossip. I want to be a good example for God. His moral excellence, integrity, and sincerity should exude from my being. When others talk to me, they should walk away thinking, *Now there's a nice, happy, thoughtful, or perceptive person. Didn't she say she's a Christian?*

We should be a walking, talking, breathing advertisement that living for God is really living!

Personal Reflections

Some things that make me angry are:

_____

_____

_____

_____

Different ways I can express my feelings other than shouting:

_____

_____

_____

_____

16
Being Rigid is Wretched

⁕

*D*ear God:

How I love all Your marvelous creations! If You made something that I do not understand, You always cast Your light on it and bring awareness by teaching me a wonderful lesson.

I have a tree in my yard that I never cared for. All the times I studied it, I could not fathom what it was about the tree that bothered me. Then one day, while I was outside with my dogs, I asked You why I did not like that particular tree. Then I realized that this tree has one branch where all the shoots grow straight up. Even the shoots on the underside of this branch grew in the same fashion. It looked so unnatural and odd. But why did it bother me so much?

In my heart, I could hear You conveying to me: "You are a lot like this branch. In trying to obtain things in your own strength (instead of giving things to Me), you can become rigid like this branch. At some point, this branch was not getting the light it needed and contorted itself to reach the sun. It is the same way with man. When you force things to happen in your own strength, instead of yielding to Me, You become rigid like that branch. You are *trying* to be, rather than just submitting to Me."

When I try to make things happen by doing in my own strength, instead of turning it over to God, I make myself the center of my universe. This is a dangerous place to be.

> So then [God's gift] is not a question of human will
> and human effort, but of God's mercy. [It depends
> not on one's own willingness nor on his strenuous
> exertion as in running a race, but on God's having
> mercy on him.] (Rom. 9:16 AMP)

Now I am at a point in my life where I want the very best God
has for me. All my life I settled for "seconds," and I now realize I
compromised (which originates from low self- esteem). I thought I
was not deserving simply because I felt I was of the least. Jesus said,
"Whatever you do to the *least* of my brothers, you do to Me." That
also includes what I think and speak about myself. I must be kind to
myself and embrace the truth that I am "the righteousness of God in
Him [Christ]" (2 Cor. 5:21 NKJV).

Being rigid in my mind and my mouth hinders God from working
with me. Because of my free will, He will not force me to do anything.
He can show me the right way only if I submit to Him.

I have consciously chosen to be the way God wants me to be.
I now ask for His will to be done in my life. I want more of Him
and less of me. Sometimes it's painful, especially when it involves
changing a lifelong habit. One day I was going through withdrawal
from quitting cigarettes. I cried out loud to God in the car, "OK,
God, what do You want me to do now? I'm doing what You want
me to do!"

Then I clearly heard God say, "*No. I* am doing what *you* asked *Me*
to do. You asked for more of Me and less of you."

Shedding my mortal skin (fleshly desires) is not easy. Anything
of eternal worth and value almost always presents a challenge. But if
I am to be a living testimony of God's love in action, I must submit
to God and accept the challenge. If I am uncertain about what to do
next, I say, "Lord, let Your will be done in my life, as it is in heaven."
He always guides me to the right path. If I stray and try to do it
my way, I repent and get back on track. No, I am not perfect. I am
forgiven by His grace!

Everyday, as I center on God's way and will for my life, I become
less and less like that rigid tree. Sure, I have times of falling short

and feeling inept. But that's why I need God to help me get up and back on track again. The key is in knowing it's not just *me* anymore. God in me makes *we*, and with that partnership comes endless possibilities.

Father:

Help me by daily reminding me that a lot people are in hell singing the same song: "I Did It My Way." God, I need You to get through my day, to make wise choices, to love no matter what. I rely upon You to live. My next breath is dependant upon You.

Help me to never walk in the pride and selfishness that only leads into further sin. I want more of You and less of me. Knowing You more is the key. In Jesus' name.

Personal Reflections

Some ways I see I was rigid:

_____

_____

_____

I realize now I especially need God in my life to help with these weaknesses:

_____

_____

_____

My daily heartfelt prayer to God is:

_____

_____

_____

17
Giving is Really Living

Dear God:

As I learn to walk the journey You pave for me, You teach me to move over and share the road with others.

At times I must walk alone, and those are the times for growth. I now know walking with You, Lord, means continually giving freely of myself.

Bringing my relationship full circle with You, walking in the fullness of it, requires endless love for others.

The life gift You provide for me can be likened to a huge gift box. Inside that box are other boxes. Those are not for me to keep. I must use each box to give to others with the same love my box is given. As I give these gifts, it is up to each recipient to look inside and realize the purpose for its contents. If I have the love of God in my heart, I will know exactly what to do. This is how God's legacy of love is carried on.

I have heard it said, "Love is a present you give to yourself." This is so true because it lines up with God's rule of "seedtime and harvest." When I give of my love, time, money, etc., I plant a seed. In time I will see a harvest. Sometimes it is not instantaneous. Perhaps at those times God teaches me a lesson in patience or helps me to mature spiritually. Being nice to those who are nice to me is easy.

The challenge begins when I return love for hatred, bitterness for gentleness, patience for rudeness.

> But the fruit of the [Holy] Spirit [the work
> which His presence within accomplishes] is love,
> joy (gladness), peace, patience (an even temper,
> forbearance), kindness, goodness (benevolence),
> faithfulness, gentleness (meekness, humility), self-
> control (self-restraint, continence). Against such
> things there is no law [that can bring a charge].
> (Gal. 5:22–23 AMP).

Giving is what causes me to grow. It also helps me to mature by opening my eyes to see beyond myself.

When I dwell on situations I have no control over, it begins a vicious cycle of worry and torment, which only leads to more worry and torment. Jesus asked, "And who of you by worrying and being anxious can add one unit of measure (cubit) to his stature or to the span of his life?" (Matt. 6:27 AMP).

This kind of "selfness" does no good for me. In a sense I say, "I have to carry this problem because I am more capable at handling it than God." Doesn't this sound like walking in pride? I should know that pride goes before a fall (Prov. 16:18). A prime example is in Hosea where Israel's *pride* and *self-reliance* cause them to fall.

> But the pride and self-reliance of Israel testifies
> before his [own] face. Therefore shall [all] Israel,
> and [especially] Ephraim [the northern ten tribes],
> totter and fall in their iniquity and guilt, and Judah
> shall stumble and fall with them. (Hosea 5:5 AMP)

If I realize and identify my actions as they really are—willful self-righteousness and disobedience to God—I can take measures to change my perspective.

Through God, I can learn to take the focus off my circumstances and see the broader picture. When I am about God's business, He will be about mine.

I need to comprehend that God is all knowing, all powerful, and best equipped to solve my problems. Moreover, He commands me to give Him *all* my cares.

> Casting the whole of your care [all your anxieties,
> all your worries, all your concerns, once and for all]
> on Him, for He cares for you affectionately and
> cares about you watchfully. (1 Pet. 5:7 AMP)

In casting all my cares upon God, I take a giant step of faith. I believe and hold to His promise that He *will* supply my every need. I continue to walk in faith by holding fast to His Word. When I study God's Word daily, I engrave His promises upon my heart and mind. In doing this, I remain strengthened and empowered, well equipped for anything that would come my way.

Father:

Help me to know without a doubt, You are in control! You care for my every need because You care for me. Your Word says You hold all of us in Your mighty hand, and nothing and no one can remove us from Your mighty grasp. Help to calm any anxieties and fears I may have, by instilling in me Your shalom, Your peace. I ask the Holy Spirit (the Helper) to come to my aid and comfort my heart and mind. In Jesus' name.

Personal Reflections

I have total confidence and I feel assured that God is changing the following areas of my life:

_____   _____

_____   _____

_____   _____

_____   _____

Things that previously caused me to fear but now "through Christ I am more than a conqueror":

_____   _____

_____   _____

_____   _____

_____   _____

Being "transformed" to me means:

_____

_____

_____

Being a new creature in Christ means "old things have passed away, all things are new." In what ways am I beginning to see God's "newness" in my life?

_____

_____

_____

18

Seeing Yourself as God Sees You

*D*ear God:

As I am growing and maturing in Your knowledge and love, I find myself also increasing in confidence. In the past, I always saw myself as someone who was just mediocre, a basic so-so person. Now the more time I spend in relationship with You, the more I realize just who I am—someone created a little lower than the angels, crowned with glory and honor, and given dominion over the works of His hands. (Ps. 8:4–6)

Knowing who I am in God can make the difference between just getting by and soaring to great heights! Realizing God's desires for my life can change my whole perspective. My attitude determines my altitude!

Many people in the Bible got a revelation of who they were in God. Doing so changed the course of their lives and history too.

David, through walking closely with God, conquered the giant, Goliath. Though he was just a young boy, his faith in God was bigger than all the soldiers of Israel. With one shot from a simple sling, he subdued and killed the mighty giant. It was not by David's might or power but by God's Spirit (connected with David's faith), which slew the Philistine.

In reading 1 Samuel, you will discover God had been preparing David for this battle all along. David confidently declared, "The Lord Who delivered me out of the paw of the lion and out of the paw of the bear, He will deliver me out the hand of this Philistine" (1 Sam. 17:37 AMP).

Through walking in obedience to God and remaining faithful, David was fulfilling the plan God had for his life.

As I study David, Abraham, Moses, Noah, Joseph, and others, I began to see the connection between obeying God and ascending to great heights.

When they walked in rebellion and self-righteousness, they reaped great sadness and regret. Remember, there is no testimony without first a test.

Being human, I must fend off many thoughts each day. None of us is perfect and never will be until we shed these bodies and dwell with God in heaven. Many times little hills of unrealistic expectations grow into huge mountains by dwelling on the same thoughts over and over again. I must recognize the enemy will use these false impressions to try to bring me into a place where darkness dwells and trap me there.

My weight has challenged me over the past fifteen years. I had found myself looking in the mirror and thinking or saying things such as, "You are disgusting! You are so fat! You're ugly!" The list continued. I had learned not to say negative things about other people, places, and things, but I thought it was all right to entertain such thoughts about myself.

One day God showed me I was not my own, but I was bought with a price (1 Cor. 6:19–20). Moreover, God commands all of us to not disgrace ourselves nor be put to shame in anything (Phil. 1:20).

**I am not yet where I want to be,
but I know God is never finished with me!**

Knowing who I am in Christ and confessing the Word will bring me out of the miry clay and plant me on the rock.

When I can fully comprehend how much He loves me, I can appreciate that God *is* love and He can be nothing else (1 John 4:7–21). Through communion with God, His love is brought to full completion. It is a perfect love.

Only when I walk out of God's perfect will do I stumble and fall. It is up to me to repent and go back to God.

He welcomes me with open arms and tosses my iniquities into the sea of forgetfulness, never to be seen again. But I must seek first the kingdom and His righteousness and all things will be given to me (Matt. 6:33).

Heavenly Father:

Thank you for all Your wondrous gifts. I am blessed beyond measure by Your perfect love. Help me to better comprehend Your love and be a living example of it by walking in it everyday. Use Your love to restore the years of hurt in me. Build me up to where I am confident and resourceful, better equipped for Your work in the kingdom. I am at my best when I serve You. In Jesus' name.

Personal Reflections

Some ways I see myself growing (maturing) with God:

_____

_____

_____

Seeing this change proves to me I know who I am in Christ. So who am I?

_____

_____

_____

19

Endure—Remain Strong!

Dear God:

For the first time in my life, I can honestly say I have the victory!

This is not to say I do not encounter trials and adversity, but I am boldly confessing, "No longer will trials overtake me."

The word *endure* in the original Bible text means to "remain strong." Jesus and the apostles were in a boat when a violent storm approached, and the men feared for their lives (Matt. 8:23–26). Jesus continued to *rest in the storm* until the apostles woke Him. Jesus rebuked them by saying, "Why are you timid and afraid, O you of little faith?" (v. 26 AMP). When Jesus called them "of little faith," He did not mean small in proportion (size); He meant little in regard to duration (time passed). "God has dealt to each one a measure of faith" (Rom. 12:3 NKJV). The key to access faith and develop it is to read and study God's Word. It's also vital to pray and commune with God every day so "that He may grant you a spirit of wisdom and revelation [of insights into mysteries and secrets] in the [deep and intimate] knowledge of Him, by having the eyes of your heart flooded with light, so you can know and understand the hope to which He has called you, and how rich is His glorious inheritance in the saints (His set apart ones) (Eph. 1:17–18 AMP)."

As Jesus awoke and rebuked the wind, I must also wake from my complacency to address situations in my life. Jesus spoke to the storm, "Shalom, be still!"

The word *shalom* means peace. But the original Hebrew greeting means to be safe, be well, be happy, have health, have prosperity, as well as to be at peace. I would say that just about covers everything.

Knowing this, I will strive to acquire this "God peace," not by toiling in my own strength but by continually abiding in Him.

> You will guard him and keep him in perfect and
> constant peace whose mind [both its inclination and
> its character] is stayed on You, because he commits
> himself to You, leans on You, and hopes confidently
> in You. (Isa. 26:3 AMP)

> Peace I leave with you; My [own] peace I now give
> and bequeath to you. Not as the world gives do
> I give to you. Do not let your hearts be troubled,
> neither let them be afraid. (John 14:27 AMP)

It is time to speak to life's storms, "Shalom, be still!" I will not be afraid. I will remember my tongue is a mighty vessel of power. As long as I profess (speak) defeat over the storms, I will continue to tie the hands of God.

I used to feel silly speaking, "Shalom, be still" over my circumstances, but I did it anyhow. What power there is in speaking God's Word.

Here is an exercise I practice: I find the best place to speak to the storms. Whether it be the bathroom or the basement, the yard or the car (my favorite spot); I'll pick a spot and speak to the mountain. I will see results. God will always deliver.

My message to mountain: Move!

> For truly I say to you, if you have faith [that is
> living] like a grain of mustard seed, you can *say* to

this mountain, Move from here to yonder place, and it will move; and nothing will be impossible to you. (Matt. 17:20 AMP)

Father:

I thank You that I am delivered out of darkness into Your wonderful light! I thank You for giving me the courage to carry on victoriously, to speak to the storms of my life with boldness by saying, "Shalom, be still!" I praise You for teaching me Your principles, and I hold them close to my heart. I confess I will use them every day to stave off all the attacks of the enemy on my life. I will continue to confess Your Word out loud and study to show myself approved. I thank You, Father, I have been given special favor through Your Son, Jesus Christ. I will never take this privilege for granted. In Jesus' name.

Personal Reflections

I speak "shalom" to these storms:

_____

_____

_____

The place I chose to speak to the storms is:

_____

Why?

_____

_____

The following mountains are moving:

_____

_____

_____

20
Victory!

Dear God:

  This is the final but the most important chapter of this book. This message is for a loving Father who always gives His children another chance at life. I cannot convey in words how much love and appreciation I feel for You, Lord. But if You look inside my heart, You will see the love and witness the depth of my emotions. Yet it will never come close to the love You have for me and all Your children.

  I pray, Lord, everyone reading this book will see the light of Your love reflected in their own eyes and the beauty that accompanies that love. They will seek out and discover You and thereby find the purpose You have for their existence. That all will climb out from the pit of despair, where circumstances have held them captive, and realize their worth through Your guidance and mercy.

  You have proved to me (a rehabilitated nobody) that You can take whom the world calls undeserving, undesirable, unworthy, and mold them into "a child of the King" through the precious blood of Your Son, Jesus Christ.

  I pray all those reading this book will comprehend the gifts our heavenly Father has in store if we only hearken to His voice. Know the voice that has haunted you all your life does not belong to God. May you recognize the great difference between His sweet whispers of encouragement and the condemning tones of a dragon whose only desire is to keep you bound.

You are not alone! Jesus shed His precious blood to ensure you will never have to be in darkness or seclusion. If you find you are presently in a state of sadness and despair, run to Him. He is ever waiting with arms wide open. His love is never cold. He will never reject you. He wants only the best for you—God's best.

If anyone reading this book desires to "walk the path of light" and has not yet received Jesus Christ as Savior, please take a moment and read this prayer out loud:

> Dear God, I confess that I am a sinner and am sorry for all the wrongs that I have done. I believe that Your Son, Jesus Christ, died on the cross for my sins. Please forgive me. I invite You, Jesus, to come into my heart and life as Lord and Savior. I commit and trust my life to You. Please give me the desire to be what You want me to be and to do what You want me to do. Thank You for dying for my sins, for Your free pardon, for Your gift of eternal life, and for hearing and answering my prayer. Amen.

If you have read this prayer, know this: The best is yet to come! You now are a member of the most exclusively blessed club in the universe! There is no way to go but up! You are an overcomer by the blood of the Lamb and the words of your testimony.

God in me spells V-I-C-T-O-R-Y!

> But thanks be to God, Who gives us the victory [making us conquerors] through our Lord Jesus Christ. (1 Cor. 15:57 AMP)

Appendix

Prayers

I have combined several scriptures into the following prayers in order to use God's Word as a tool to pray effectively. I hope you will see as many benefits as I have since I started praying them out loud daily.

Place your name, or the names of others, in the blanks.

Prayer for Self

O Lord, God of Israel, grant unto me, this very day, the prayer and petitions I ask of You:

Let ____ be like a tree firmly planted beside the waters. Let ___ be healthy and flourish like the palm tree; long lived, upright, useful, and fruitful. ____ shall grow like a cedar in Lebanon—majestic, stable, durable, and incorruptible.

You, Lord, are ____ high tower and defense, and ____ God, the rock of ____ refuge. ____ dwells in the secret place of the most high

God and remains stable and fixed under the shadow of the Almighty, Whose power no foe can withstand. You deliver ____ from the snare of the fowler and from the deadly pestilence. ____ shall not be afraid of the terror of night, nor the wicked and evil plots that fly by day. Let the beauty and delightfulness and favor of You be upon ____. Establish the works of ____ hands and let Your works be revealed in ____.

____ soul yearns for the courts of the Lord. ____ heart and flesh cry out and sing for joy to You, O God. ____ will bless You, Lord, at all times. Your praise shall continue to be in ____ mouth. You redeem the life of Your servant, and none who takes refuge and trust in You will be condemned. You give ____ beauty for ashes. You have turned _____ mourning into dancing. You gird ____ with gladness. You give ____ unyielding and impenetrable strength. Your favor is for a lifetime and in Your favor, Lord, is life!

Surely only goodness and mercy will follow ____ all the days of ____ life, and the house of the Lord and Your presence is _____ dwelling place. In Jesus' name. Amen.

Prayer for Family and Friends

My family (and/or) friends _____ shall serve the Lord all of their days, and great shall be their peace. Unto You, Lord, I bring their lives. They are the generation who seek Your face. You are their Shepherd, and they shall not lack. You forgive all of their sins, and they dwell in the refuge of Your strength. With long life they will be satisfied, and they will dwell in Your house forever. You will bear them up lest they dash their foot against a stone. You give Your angels charge over them, and they will show forth all your marvelous works and wonderful deeds.

Create in _____ a clean heart, O God, and renew a right, persevering, and steadfast spirit in them. _____ shall be like a tree planted by the waters that spreads out their roots by the river;

and they will not see and fear when heat comes; but they will be joyful. _____ will not be anxious and full of care in the year of drought, nor shall they cease yielding fruit.

Thank You, Lord, that _____ seek first Your kingdom and Your righteousness, and all provisions will be given to them. _____ will not worry about tomorrow, but they will press on in Your peace that passes all understanding.

_____ put on the full armor of God, that they are able to stand against all the strategies of the devil. _____ put on the belt of truth, the breastplate of right standing with You, God. _____ feet are shod with the preparation of the gospel of peace. _____ lift up their shield of faith to quench the fiery darts of the wicked; _____ put on the helmet of salvation and they uphold the sword of the Spirit, which is Your holy Word.

_____ will continually pray at all times in the Spirit, for the earnest, heartfelt prayer of Your righteous people makes tremendous power available (dynamic in its working), and we draw our strength from You, Lord.

I thank You, Lord, that through skillful and godly wisdom is our house built (our lives, our homes, our families), and by knowledge shall its chambers [of every area] be filled with all precious and pleasant riches.

I pray the eyes of _____'s heart flooded with light, so they can know and understand that hope to which He has called us; and how rich is His glorious inheritance for us who believe. In Jesus' name. Amen.

Journaling

Healing prayers of Love/ Psalms of Peace

Oh Lord, God of heaven,
Infuse me with Your strength,
Guard me from temptation,
Shower me with grace.
Cause my lips to speak Your truths,
The words of life, not death,
Let me use your Word for food,
To nourish me again.
Restore this mind of flesh anew,
And see things through Your eyes,
Rain upon this flesh with You,
Cleanse me from all pride.
Relinquish all, this carnal being,
Transcend my spirit higher,
So, I may sing like angels sing,
Consumed by holy fire.

Psalms 63:8 My whole being follows hard after You and clings closely to You; Your right hand upholds me.

When I have these days so bleak,
I do not think You have forgotten me.
It is at these times, I realize,
You are with me the most.
I feel You close,
Breathing on me,
Caressing me,
Whispering in my spirit's ear,
"I am here, do not despair."
I feel the warmth right from Your palm,
Your Love and peace, how blanket-soft.

*II Corinthians 1:3 Blessed be the God and Father of our Lord Jesus Christ, the Father of sympathy (pity and mercy) and the God [Who is the source] of every comfort (consolation and encouragement), Who comforts us in every trouble, so that we may also be able to comfort those who are in any kind of trouble or distress, with the comfort with which we ourselves are comforted by God.

As I sat beneath the sorrow
That laid so heavy on my life,
I had sacrificed countless joys,
I had seen too many nights,
The pain has cost me years of rain,
Took youth and years from me,
Within mere seconds my heart and head
Had quite a wakening.
God's Spirit was amid my thoughts,
He brought to my attention,
The years I spent in agony,
This wasn't God's rejection.
He'd beckon me with a quiet voice,
"Come out of your despair,"
But, I felt as though I'd not a choice,
I was resigned to stay right there.
I silenced His call with pity and strife,
Ignoring his comfort and Love,
All the while, He stayed close beside,
Waiting 'till I had enough.
In desperation I cried out loud,
I fell upon my knees,
"Help me, God. Help me now,
Father, can you hear me?"
And then He spoke to me,
In a quiet, calming tone,
"Now, are you ready?
I've been waiting all along."

Psalms 145:18 The Lord is near to all who call upon Him, to all who call
upon Him sincerely and in truth.

I feel the breath of life spring forth,
I sense it is time to grow,
I must ascend to a higher course,
Where living waters flow.
The climb may take a rocky turn,
But God will see me through,
He gives me hind's feet, swift and sure,
I'll not be tripped or moved.
His well, my source of strength awaits,
To quench, when I must drink,
He takes me from the earthen clay,
To the rock, so I won't sink.
When a storm is drawing near,
I hide beneath the cleft,
The load is light enough to bear,
Under His wings, He gives me rest.
The sun's hot rays won't scorch or hurt,
In the shadow of His love,
His refuge waits at every turn,
His grace, much more than enough.
My destiny, His secret place,
His glory greets me there,
In quiet, I am warm and safe,
I speak to God in prayer.

Psalms 91:1 He who dwells in the secret place of the most high shall remain stable and fixed under the shadow of the Almighty [Whose power no foe can withstand].

God is covering His earth with a blanket of His Love. He stands at every point and echoes words of life, setting forth growth, provision, and abundance. See His works in the mighty things He is bringing to pass: The green grass, the leaves on the trees, the flowers, showing their marvelous colors; He gives us rainbows everyday. A promise of a new thing, new creations to behold. As long as we look with spiritual eyes wide open, we will witness His glory, His splendor, His majesty. Everywhere, we will see His face.

Job 42:5 I had heard of You [only] by the hearing of the ear, but now my [spiritual] eye sees You.

>+•>•O•<•+<

I am growing in the knowledge of Your love,
I am passionate beyond measure for You,
I am still and know you are God,
I embrace this lovely truth.
I know if I die tomorrow,
I feel in the depths of my heart,
I will not have regret,
For this life I have left,
Is a blink of an eye to You,
I stand in awe of You.

Job 13:11 Shall not His majesty make you afraid, and should not your awe for Him restrain you?

In the stillness of the evening, I fix my sites upon Your goodness and
glory,
I fight back the sleep from my eyes to write of this great story.
I will magnify Your name and speak of Your mysteries,
As only one who carries You, Your love life, deep within me.
I breathe in Your nature and will raise my hands to praise you,
I will shout Your name on high and sing of Your wondrous nature.
Let all be aware of Your magnificence and let all Your children unite,
For our Father is glorious and He inhabits all our cries.

Psalms 27:6 I will sing, yes I will sing praises to the Lord.

Oh Lord, You are glorious and magnificent,
All praise belongs to You. Almighty is the Lamb.
You are the same yesterday, today, and tomorrow,
And Your endless blessings carry no sorrow.
I bring all the wounds, the bruises of this life,
I lay them at Your feet, You heal me with Your sighs.
You challenge me to change myself,
Transcending me to Your life-filled well.
I once was lost, but now I am found,
I was tattered and in pieces, I am covered by You now.
I bow down and remain humbled by Your sight,
I wait for Your guidance; in You, I will abide.
Like the deer who pants for water,
I will long for You evermore, my Father.

Ephesians 4:24 And put on the new nature (the regenerate self) created in
God's image, [Godlike] in True righteousness and holiness.

Please don't take value in this vapor,
It is not long before it's dust,
If you strive to mingle in your measure,
You will watch it corrode and rust.
Hearts, calloused by the laboring
Of striving in our strength,
Will be softened by one measuring
Of God's goodness and His grace.
The real value is the One that brings eternal life to you,
Without Jesus, things die and fade; With Him, all things are new.

Ecclesiastes 2:11 Then I looked on all that my hands had done and the labor
I had spent in doing it, and behold, all was vanity and a striving after the
wind and a feeding on it, and there was no profit under the sun.

⋗─◆──○──◆─⋖

In the midst of a tender moment,
While I seek having You ever more,
I seize and respond to Your calling,
Your waves billow onto my shore.
I drift in Your water, it soothes me,
I proclaim it is all that I need,
I bask in the wondrous breaking,
Of Your healing and tender springs.
The water is ever rising,
But I need not to swim or strive,
I wade in Your marvelous tidings,
I just float and I close my eyes.

John 4:14 But the water that I will give him shall become a spring of water
welling up (flowing, bubbling) [continually] within him unto (into, for)
eternal life.

To all who labor upon this earth,
Who feel downcast and unwanted,
To those who rarely have felt the warmth
Of kind words when it really counted.
I wanted to give you this message of hope,
From the One Who knows your name,
He has seen all the times you had been so low,
He is there, He can feel your pain.
He was there all the nights your pillow was soaked,
With tears when you felt no one cared,
When loved ones reject you and you think you're alone,
He wants you to know, He is there.
He sees all the people, the ones we don't see,
They are home alone, or they're out on the street.
And you don't have to be poor,
To be in utter despair,
All the money in this world,
Won't bring happiness near.
This message, I give you,
Is one of new hope,
He is there, can you see Him?
He sees you, He knows.
He was poor and neglected,
He has felt all your pain,
He felt despised and rejected
By the very people He saved.
Though we continue to hurt Him,
We hate and we sin,
He'll continue to reach out,
To draw us closer to Him.
He knows all of us,
He knows us by name,
Just reach out and trust Him,
You will smile once again.

Hebrews 2:18 For because He Himself has suffered in being tempted, He is able to run to the cry of those who are being tempted and tested and tried.

In the stillness of Your glory,
I see the goodness of Your ways,
I see myself enduring,
Though the storms may come my way.
I've exchanged my strength for Your strength,
I am covered by Your love,
Your mercy, it sustains me,
Though the going may get rough.
I see the path ahead now,
Your brilliance lights my way,
I am calmed by Your lovely heart sounds,
I 'm secure in Your strong embrace.
Life's troubles, they are fleeting,
What is now, will soon be gone,
But God's love is ever with me,
Through His presence, I stand strong.

Ephesians 3:20 Now to Him by the power that is at work within us, is able to do superabundantly, far over and above all we ask or think.

I take your hand gently in Mine,
Your smile so real, I can see your heart,
I see Myself in your soft eyes.
I see how the years have brought you hurt,
But I see past all those signs;
I only see what you deserve.
I dance to the beat of your heartstrings,
I follow your lead as we twirl;
I smile as you sing in my ear.
I caress your heart
And healing comes.
I love you, little girl.
We don't need to talk,
Our language transcends words,
I hear your mind whispering,
"Once more Jesus, Once more,"
"Do not worry, my child,
This dance goes on and on,
Let us dance now in your dreams,
To the Spirit's own sweet song.

Psalm 118:14 The Lord is my Strength and Song; and He has become my Salvation.

Breathe on me Lord, Your sweet breath of life,
Lay upon this heart, Your tender strength,
With the help of my God, I cast off all concerns,
I will not have too much to bear.
I see You approach, near the wings of my soul,
The wind of Your Spirit clears my thoughts,
I lay, refreshed on the breeze You've created,
I recline in the hollow of Your hand.
Your love surrounds my whole being,
I 'm not afraid, with You I will stand.
You have not disappointed, nor pushed me aside,
I am healed because of You.
I live because You love.

Psalm 57:1 Yes, in the shadow of Your wings will I take refuge and be confident until calamities and destructive storms are passed.

Many in the "garden of life" would call you a "weed,"
But I have called you to be a "wildflower;"
Whose roots grow deep in the hardest of soils,
And leaf will not wither in the heat and storms.
Some will cut you off or hoe you down,
But you grow back ever strong.
Man has not brought you to this place,
Nor will man take you away.
You will spread out and multiply
As My Word was spoken, My Word cannot lie.
I will take you to the higher ground,
For you were planted by the hand of God.

Jeremiah 17:8 For he shall be like a tree planted by the waters that spreads out its roots by the river; and it shall not see and fear when heat comes; but its leaf shall be green.

In the time of a sweet,
Sweet second,
We will have a revelation,
And nothing is the same,
When we realize His grace.
At the moment
our eyes have opened,
We can see the path before us;
With clarity, awareness,
He creates a light to lead us.
What best describes this "glory,"
While I stumbled in clay, miry,
Then He sent
A light my way,
You, my God created "day."

Psalm 112:4 Light arises in the darkness for the upright, gracious, compassionate, and just [who are in right standing with God].

><+>—O—<+><

One thing that I know,
One thing I am sure of,
I will dwell in His house forever,
And rest in His abundance.
I will stand as the new day breaks forth,
To gaze on all His creation,
I will submit to His voice,
Ever calling,
And sing praises for my salvation.

Psalm 84:10 For a day in Your courts is better than a thousand [anywhere else].

I am sitting and weaving a new life for you,
A life full of blessings and love,
I carefully guide all the tread through life's loom,
I'm so happy 'cause I love this job.
The thread that I'm using is silver and gold,
For you are precious to Me, don't you see?
So do not feel weary and do not get low,
I will carry you through everything.
The life that you knew,
The heartache and pain,
Are a thing of the past for you,
So stand and believe,
All things are changed,
Behold, I make all things brand new.

Ephesians 4:24 Put on the new nature (the regenerate self) created in
God's image, [Godlike] in true righteousness and holiness.

As I gazed at the mirror in the darkness,
With strained eyes, I labored to see,
The one you created, an image,
But night's shadows enveloped me.
I stood back and I pondered this vision,
(Or the lack of a vision, I'd say),
I prayed for a better depiction,
The next time I looked on my face.
I heard a clear voice in the dimness,
One that shattered my ebony sky,
"Are you waiting to make your own brightness,
For only I 'll bring you out of the night."
"Come to Me, all of you, that are laden,
I've a candle to light your way,
I'm a beacon to those who are wayward,
I'm the One who turns night into day."

Psalm 112:4 Light arises in the darkness for the upright, gracious,
compassionate, and just [who are in right standing with God].

My friends,
I do not know you
In the sense of familiarity,
But I am no stranger
To pain and adversity;
I have tasted bitter sorrows,
Felt the sting of life's tomorrows.
If I could give you
One message of hope,
I would give you the vision,
The sight beyond our human scope.
I have witnessed rebirth
Through the ache of despair,
While I struggled in darkness,
I found a beacon of Light there.
A candle to guide
Through the darkest of nights,
God's radiance beckons,
We are healed by His Light.

In the stillness of Your glory,
I see the goodness of Your ways,
I see myself enduring,
Though the storms may come my way.
I have exchanged my strength for
Your strength,
I am covered by Your love,
Your mercy, it sustains me,
Though the going may get rough.
I see the path ahead now,
Your brilliance lights my way,
I am calmed by Your lovely heart sounds,
I 'm secure in Your strong embrace.
Life's troubles, they are fleeting,
What is now, will soon be gone,
But God's love is ever with me,*
Through His presence, I stand strong.

➤──◆──○──◆──◄

Isaiah 41:10
Fear not [there is nothing to fear], for I am with you; do not look around you in terror and be dismayed, for I am your God. I will strengthen and harden you to difficulties, yes I will help you; yes I will hold you up and retain you with My [victorious] right hand of rightness and justice.

Come to His loving table,
All you are welcome here,
Enjoy all the gifts He offers,
He waits for His children there.
The table is ever ready,
It seats countless guests every day;
Your chair is always vacant,
You need not reserve your space.
Taste all the fruits of His Spirit,
Kindness and peace He gives;
Joy upon measure is waiting,
If you only will sup with Him.
There are days when the seats are empty,
There are times He sits there with few;
But He never clears the table,
He waits at the table for YOU.

Lord, In solitude, I find Your solace.
One emotion, one prayer
Transcends another.
I become aware,
Your presence awaits there.
I follow Your voice.
Your Spirit whispers,
My heart is full.
I surrender to the serenity.
The sounds of Your Love
Echo, ever clearer,
And washing over me,
Spills,
Sweet refrains of Your grace.

The first step is the hardest.
But as the first blooms of Crocus and Tulips come forth with boldness,
Making way from the frozen earth,
Under blankets of snow,
They burst forth.
A gentle whisper of spring,
A promise of life,
Amidst an otherwise landscape of ice.
Be bold for Me.
The best is yet to come.
I will bring you out of the dormant earth,
Into the bright sun.
Open your arms, accept My embrace,
Feel the warmth of My Love upon your face.

⊱┈❀┈◦┈❀┈⊰

Oh protector of mine,
Thou art my beacon of light.
Serve as my shield in time,
Cushion my heart in plight.
Preserve this mind bent in sorrow,
Through this time...until tomorrow.

⊱┈❀┈◦┈❀┈⊰

Psalm 103
Bless the Lord, O my soul; and forget not all of His benefits–
Who forgives all your iniquities, Who heals all your diseases,
Who redeems your life from the pit and corruption, Who beautifies,
Dignifies, and crowns you with loving-kindness and tender mercy.

A candle emits a brilliant light,
It spills into the room.
If it were not for the dark of night,
We would fail to see light too.
It seems, in life, the times we hurt,
Is when we see true growth,
The realm in which our gloom exists,
Creates contrast for the glow.
A lucid awareness of our strength,
True strength that God provides,
Enduring the seasons, the times of change,
Brings renewal to our lives.

⊱┈◈┈○┈◈┈⊰

My children, the Comforter [Parakletos] is here to stay,
He will carry you from night until the dawn of a new day.
I will take you out of your despair,
In all things praise Me, I will be there.
Nothing is impossible to Me,
I am God. All I see.
Do not wallow in your grief,
You are blessed above, you are not beneath.
Evil resides in iniquities,
Cast anger aside, in love, be free.
Find strength in praise and prayer,
Cast aside all fear.
I cover you with all My grace,
In the cleft, I will renew your faith.
Let nothing and no one dwell in here,
I love you all with tender care.
Hold and embrace Me in your heart,
I will always love you. I will never stop.

In the days of thy life,
May Gods peace rest upon you.
An abundant sum to carry you on,
Through times of torment,
Roads so long,
A just measure to last your years,
His blanket of strength,
To dry your tears.
His love shall burn,
A forever light,
To pierce the darkness,
Put out the night.

Isaiah 35:2 It shall blossom abundantly and rejoice even with joy and singing.

⊳⊶⊷⊙⊶⊷⊲

Lord:

    My flesh is so weak. The trials of every day life try to break my spirit. I yearn for the Comforter to release me from these troubles.

    Oh Holy Spirit, send God's anointing to ease this pain. My body aches and my mind is filled with torment. The day is so long. I need to rest in your arms, Father. Quiet my mind and release the stress from this body. I wait to receive your Godly peace.

    I am at last, awakened to your presence. As I let go of confusion and anxiety, I become an open vessel to receive your peace and Love. I breathe in your compassion and it fills my very being with tranquility. I accept your healing touch and it renews every fiber, each cell, of my body. I bask in the knowledge I am one with You, Lord. You are my Savior, my every need in all circumstances. In you, I am healed and whole.

Come into my heart, dear Savior,
Do not tread lightly,
I await Your presence there.
Accept the many fractures, large and mite,
For many have traveled this vessel.
Sing into its chambers,
A sonnet of Your love,
It serves to mend its tender walls.
Abide in it for a time,
Your comfort will dry these tears.
Let me bask in the glow of Your love
And restore my strength.
With You, I am whole.
I have everything.
My spirit, my soul,
Echoes,
Jesus Christ the king.

⇒·┤◆►·○·◄◆├·⇐

Oh Lord, my Lord:

How I exalt thee! Thy knowledge astounds the greatest of men and sends the proud to their knees. I come before You Lord, with petitions only You can bring sense to. How very weak I feel, God. I rely solely on Your direction and I await Your blessed guidance. Come to me Lord. Only You can sustain me by Your mighty right hand. You can hide me in the shelter of Your wings and bring liberty to where I have been held captive. Gaze upon me Lord with Your healing glance. I marvel at Your excellence. Jehovah Jireh, our provider, Your grace is sufficient for me!

You are His child, His workmanship.
The price of your salvation was paid with His life.
Your eternal spirit was ransomed, signed with His blood.
The stripes on His back ensure your health and well-being.
His Love is everlasting and as perfect as His Word.
He alone changed our destiny. He lived to die for us.

⊷━◆━○━◆━⊶

Come to God's resting place and He will give you shelter. You who are heavy laden, come and drink from His spring of life. He offers all His blessings to each one of His children. Rest in the knowledge, Jesus assures us, not one is excluded unless he excludes himself. The Lord, our God offers resolutions to all His children. His love beckons us again and again. If we do not hearken to God's voice, perhaps it is because we remain closed. One can not see a good neighbor through closed doors and windows. Submit to God. He is the One who brings wonderful beginnings.

Guess Who?
I have just begun this journey,
Though I traveled many roads,
I have walked through many valleys,
But, I still have far to go.
The distance that's behind me,
Can never quite compare,
With the road that's been assigned me,
There is more to meet me there.
This labor will not take me,
Nor encompass my whole being,
I will not focus on my pain,
But dwell on Godly things.
I feel alone most all the time,
Though I know He's by my side,
It's when the road gets winding,
I sense He's there to guide.
I know there is an end somewhere,
A final destination,
Right now, at this point in time,
I pray for a vacation.
Who am I, what's my name?
Can you guess my vocation?
I'm Jesus Christ, the very one
Who lived all your emotions.

I Peter 4:1 So since Christ suffered in the flesh for us, for you, arm yourselves with the same thought and purpose [patiently to suffer rather than fail to please God

Printed in the United States
116846LV00002BA/213/P